Scary Dreams

An Anthology of the Liberian Civil War

Lekpele M. Nyamalon

Forte Publishing

First Published in 2017
Published by:

FORTE Publications
#12 Ashmun Street
Snapper Hill
Monrovia, Liberia
[+231] 88-110-6177

FORTE Publishing
7202 Tavenner Lane
208 Alexandria
VA, 22306

FORTE Press
76 Sarasit Road
Ban Pong, 70110
Ratchaburi, Thailand
[+66] 85-824-4382

http//:fortepublishing.wix.com/fppp
fortepublishing@gmail.com

This book or any portion thereof may not be reproduced or used in any manner whatsoever without the expressed written permission of the publisher except for the use of brief quotations in a book review.

Printed in the United States of America.

Copyright © 2017 LEKPELE M. NYAMALON
All rights reserved.

ISBN-10: 0994630867
ISBN-13: 978-0994630865

DEDICATION

To Peter S.T Marshall, a giant the world never got to meet. To that flame that dimmed before daylight, to the over 250,000 Liberians who lost their lives at check points, by stray bullets, through summary massacres and those young boys and girls, my age mates whose innocence got stolen forever.

Contents

PART 1 11
Haunted Years 11
1990 13
I'm Not a Politician 14
Single File 16
Sanibayla 17
Rock Your Jaw 18
Stray Bullet 19
The Rebel Incarnate 20
Curfew 21
Fendell 22
Duport Road 23
You Rode My Back to Power 24
Pointed Fingers 26
The Check Point 27
Behind the Doors 28
April Again 29
I Was an Advocate 30
The Beach as a Witness 32
Your Country is Mine 34
Tanzania Base 36
Masked In Darkness 37
Leave the Line 38
Midnight in July 40
The Ghost of April 12 42
Corruption 43
Diamonds 44
I Wouldn't Be, If You Didn't 46
Loguato 48
The African Soldier 49
Again? 50
Are They Still Here? 52
God Bless You? 54
September 9 55
G2 56
Freedom Fighter 57
14 Road 58

Wigs of Terror 59
Flames in the Air 60
they are coming 61
who born soldier 62
What's Your Tribe? 63
17 boots 64
Caldwell 65
Palm Cabbage 66
Carter's Camp 67
Memories of a Lonely Prisoner 68
Nov 2 69
Jungle Warriors 70
Totota 71
The White Helmet Shot My Brother 72
Sept 23 73
Smokes in Gbarnga 74
Trek to Ganta 75
Kokoya Road 76
Mae Davis 77
The Peacekeeper 78
He was Dancing 79
April 6 80
Bulk Challenge 81
I have Worn Scars 82
Note 83
When Ebola Hits Home 84
A Liberian, not Ebola 86
Ebola, Go Away 88
Blocked Gates 90
When Ebola Leaves 92
Screams from the ETU 93

PART 2 94
Exile Screams 94
Danane! 96
Landlord 98
La Marie 99
If I Went Back Today 100
Nimba Voyage 102
The Telephone booth 103
Put My Number In 104
The Resettlement Interview 105
Distribution Site 106
PMRC 107

PART 3 108
Stolen Innocence 108
They Took My Daughter 110
Double-Edged 111
Broken Rose 112
Marriage at Twilight 113
I Wanted to Be 114
My Brother Died Living 115
Massaquoi-taa 116
You Dumped Us 118
Small Soldier 119
He's Only 5 120

PA RT 4 121
Hope for the Future 121
When the Ancestors Return 123
On the Back of History 124
Vision 2030 126
Gbarnga Again! 128
You are Lifted! 130
Lift Liberia 131
Promise 132
My Country is Mine! 134
My Country, Your Country, 1 Country! 135
One Race, One Blood One Liberia 136
I Found My Compass 138
I Celebrate a Soldier 139
Unification Time 140
Red, White and Blue 141
Let's Forget [Reconciliation Poem] 142
Tribute Pieces 144
Thank you Yah (To be read in Kpelleh) 145
Tribute to all those who Died During the Civil Conflict 147
Bonus 151
Note to a Virgin, ... 152
For the Girl Child… 153
ABOUT THE AUTHOR 154

ACKNOWLEDGMENTS

To the glory of God Almighty, through whom all blessings flow. I want to say a special thanks to my father, mentor and role model, Mulbah G. Nyamalon (sainted memory), a dedicated professional and educator, for all the sacrifices he made to give me the light and for teaching me how to dream.

Thanks to my mother, Belekula Dennis Jeogbor for her prayers and always being there.

To my elder sister, Guladia, who walked this journey with me and lived every part of the stories I share in this collection.

To Nyamah, my younger sister who survived the plane raids in Firestone. To Nyeille, our youngest sister, for her warm laughter and support.

To my daughter Leemu, for her patience to allow me to write; to my little boy, Joe, whose birth reminds me that a generation is here.

To the Rev. Moses T. Jeogbor for his prayers.

To my friend, Moyo Larmie. Thank you.

To the generation of writers before us, whose writings paved the way and for their inspiration.

Finally, to my publisher, D. Othniel Forte, who has agreed to walk with me as I unveil my story to the world, in stages.

Author's Note

I was six years old when the civil war broke out in my country Liberia. I still remember walking on the red laterite road in Massaquoi ta, my mother's village where we had gone on a family vacation, after Sunday Church Service when the news of an invasion in Nimba Country, north-central Liberia, had taken International airwaves. I remember the aftereffects of the civil war, the many nightmares I had, the fear of death, the hunger, the hunt for palm kernels, Borbor Johns, Kissmes [pronounced as Kiss Mes].

I remember that moment when my mother had to shield me from that rebel with the nom de guerre 'General Dirty Water'* who had asked me to hold his 'sister' Beretta handgun.

Scary Dreams is an attempt to paint a picture of those fainted memories, told from my lens, as a child, using the power of poetry to write a story of over 14 years of carnage that engulfed my country and left a nation bruised after a decade of self-destruction and neglect. May generations after us come and read that children growing up in conflict can also tell their stories, no matter how faint, in some way, they too can put a dot in the lines of a story of how conflicts affect their lives. The poems in this collection are personal experiences of the author, experiences of others whose voices drowned, or sank too low to speak, but I'm glad that they are able to tell their stories through mine.

May the vices that led us to carnage and destruction never lift their heads again and may we as a people learn from the wreckage of wars that we should never again, tear ourselves apart as we did. May this glorious land of Liberty, long remain ours. God bless Liberia!

* The name was changed because it was too profane

Scary Dreams

A shout in thin air
Hurried away by the breeze
Scary dreams linger

PART 1

Haunted Years

Bruised by anarchy
Sieged in the wings of terror
The years faded thin

1990

1990…
It was 1990
the year still rings a bell
guns were blasting,
kids were crying,
all Liberia was plunged in turmoil
folks were walking line by line, from
Monrovia to Fendell, Kakata to
Gbarnga

1990...
It was 1990
the year stinks like a bee, hunger
struck Monrovia like an assigned
lightening Cholera and Diarrhea
stormed like a Hurricane

1990, I say it was 1990
The year smells
like a decomposed carcass
families lost loved ones
all in a senseless war

1990 ... but why did you ever come?
Hope your memories are buried
in the sands of time.

I'm Not a Politician

I'm not a politician,
just a woman by the stalls
that boards a truck
from Grand Gedeh to Sinoe.
Bringing my dried meat and pepper
    Oil and charcoal
    I need roads to make this work.
Does it make you angry?

I'm not a politician
just a boy sitting on stones
in Gbarpolu, in a bare
room they call a school
    I need a pencil, board and teacher
    to get the education for tomorrow.
Does it make you grouchy?

I'm not a politician just a
driver with a taxi taking
passengers to places
    gasoline is like diamonds
    with prices ever soaring
Is asking now treason?
Does it make you grumpy?

I'm not a politician
just a peasant with a head
    to ask those that lead
    to do better for my lot
Am I in trouble?
Does it make you cranky?

I'm not a politician
just a man with a chalk
laying tomorrow's bricks
by the day and you chase
    me in my ghetto by night
    like chickens? Why?
Do I make you feel prickly?

I'm not a politician
just a rookie with a microphone
picking the views of people
    from across the country
    for all to hear and heal
Does it make you ornery?

Single File

We lined up
holding everything we had-
    mattresses and bags
    chickens and goats-
dreaming perhaps
they would spare us.

We gave anything
they wanted...
    our food and water
    our dignity and respect
yet, like weeds on the wayside,
they picked some for the river

They took everything!
Posing as owners of life.
    men begged for their lives
    from those holding the guns;
from butchers now judges
from hunters now soldiers.

Sanibayla

Sanibayla. Oh Sanibayla!
Found deep in the Bong forest
you saved lives during the war
by hiding us deep in your pockets.
For in your lair, soldiers never dare
Folks could hide, cook their meals
in peace and even share

Sanibayla. Oh Sanibayla!
the unforgotten corner of
Zeanzue when there was famine,
you had plenty to share, for this
town, the bandits did not know the
displaced could sleep,
sound and silent,
chickens could even crow

Oh Sanibayla. Oh Sanibayla!
Thank you for your benevolence
you kept us safe in your nests at no
fare Sanibayla! Sanibayla thank you for
your time

Rock Your Jaw

Food was scarce
like gemstones
hard to come by
everyone looked drained
skinned to the last sight of ribs
feeble men like miners held shovels
shoveling the depth of the earth
searching for the prized Palm Kernels

Rock your jaw*
Rock your jaw
Rock your jaw
with Palm Kernels

The vendor's voice echoed

Everyone rushed to buy Soon
everyone was rocking taste
and money didn't matter The
strongest lived

Rock your jaws and live
Chew the strains and
Hang unto life
Rock your jaw…
The vendor sold life

*In local parlance- the act of chewing.

Stray Bullet

Come back and count
your victims
Do you know them?
Come back and recount
the carnage left in your wake
do you smile at your wreck?

You moved aimlessly you took
down giants you slayed
generations Were you on an
adventure? Perhaps a rocket
sent to space

You took down people
you never knew
fathers, mothers anyone, you
were a cannon set loose on a
task you alone knew

Go back and fetch your masters the
cowards behind the triggers who
sent you places they feared take the
guilt back to the weaklings bring
them forth or face the jury

The Rebel Incarnate

I was a rebel
my shirt color made me one
my nametag gave me a gun
I could burn a country
because I looked *funny*

While the real rebels
roamed in the forest
soldiers chased me
they hunted me down
my former protectors
now Draculas

I was the rebel incarnate the
incubator of terror because I
carried a name the soldiers
thought I could kill
while the rebels smoked our villages

I was the rebel
Why didn't I know
that my red shirt was the deal?
The soldiers feared me
even though I carried no guns
How did I become a rebel?

Curfew

For a second
I didn't know
that hours could kill

When the hours pass and doors
are shut anyone caught outside
might be put behind the bars,
where armed vampires reach
out for a sip of fresh blood

I thought soldiers fought
soldiers why did they chase me
and my brothers all around
when we had no arms to fight?

They chased us deep into the swamps
eager to tear us up for breaking the
hours; to them, we were rebels
the colors of our shirts made us rebels
the names we had were death sentences
the COs' moods, determined our fates but,
the minutes after six p.m. sealed our fates

Fendell

Fendell
the place of refuge You
were the shoreline people
sought to reach the line
that offered shelter when
chased by soldiers or the
boys in wedding gowns

You kept a basement
where people felt safe
when the marathon took us
from Sinkor to Duport Road,
we stretched our legs to
the line you stood

Holding the medals as we ran the race
passing through checkpoints manned
by drug caged boys jumping over
former friends
now turned into bodies and
skeletons Fendell, the place we hid
We longed for you,
Fendell...

Duport Road

I remember in 1990
after surviving the checkpoints
you were the 'resting place' for
countless innocent ones I
remember you

With couple of dreaded G-2
offices I remember the 'freedom
fighters' roaming
from house to house
searching for their 'targets'

you were there, silent

You sent us packing
on the long trek to Fendell
you stared at our backs as we ran
with bundles of everything we had
Duport road, you have stories to tell

You Rode My Back to Power

When you wanted power
I was an asset
you chased me in the slums
slept in the ghettos with me
asked how I slept
pretended you cared
you gave
rice
oil and
clothes
brought in containers
then, I was valuable

I rode miles for free
travelling on train
brought by my suitor
I was a princess
blind, limb or deaf
literate, semi or stark
I qualified
my thumb could do
when I was sick
you shivered
anxious to assist

you cared about me
you wiped my hand
you cleaned my eyes
you washed my feet
you treated me tender
for to you a princess I was

I could be on the streets for
hours no police dared bother
me I dare not try that
I'm now an outcast
no cars
no food
no care
no hope
my crown is gone
it was stored in my vote
I lost it like my virginity
My suitor is gone

Pointed Fingers

I looked for the assassins
behind pointed fingers
fingers that hid their hands
but said my dad was a killer
the one behind the fingers
lives with a story which one
day, we'll understand.

They lived with us
as friends and buddies
when the killers came
and the bullets went flying
The friendly fingers zoomed
in on us and told our killers,
"They are the targets!
They're the preys"
How could you do this?

In hindsight now, we know
the assassins were cowards
their fingers shut our worlds
Come out fingers!
Come face your victims!
Why did you hide your fingers?
Why did you hide your face?
Did you have to?
Did you think of today?

The Check Point

At the checkpoint,
Father threw away his
ID card shivering
At the soldier's stare
The drugged teenager
Looked at this legs
Tracing the boots mark
Death sentences
Were read aloud
By the mask wearing judge
Holding the barrel of the
AK47 as the gable
Grudges buried from ages
Resurfaced at helpless
Fleeing captives
Pleading for a breath
Stories of the checkpoints
Fill the memoirs of time
Souls fled to eternity
At the checkpoint

Behind the Doors

At the door in Accra
sat women, mothers and sisters
blocking the doors
with their hands and feet
where before all could not stop
the fist of even a child soldier
now embolden by peace
their bravery woven in courage
held the forces of warlords
locked in a room

Behind those doors were men
who at the snap of fingers
could put Liberia on fire Yet,
they stood with faith
as their sword like a hunter,
without a gun before a lion
their courage broke warlords' backs
to make the peace accord possible

April Again

It's April again
this time we have to gain
The rains are here and April is here
Troubles of old please do not dare

Our history is replete with April's woes
This time we're strong to get it off our toes
'79, '80, '96 are years of April's horror

April you have been deadly,
stealing and tearing us apart
This nation's children had
fallen, forever lost in your
clutches Now, we've risen
stronger your nightmare
Can't keep us under

It's April again,
It's April again
This time your presence
will cause us no pain.

I Was an Advocate

I brought down kingdoms
with my voice
My words were sharper
than a blade's edge.
I knew the message that
awakened the masses
That sparked the flames in their souls
I knew the cords to make them
rise to their feet in unison and chant
slogans that tore down empires

I knew the melodies that drove
the birds from the forests
and assemble them under a roof
My tongue could shake a cotton tree
throwing it to the ground
That was me... the advocate
I sit in shock and bow my face
as broken kingdoms arise and
flip their swords

I've dug a pit
and buried my feet
and sent the foot soldiers to hell
I grabbed a trumpet and blew
for emperors to conquer
on the back of the masses
and joined the melodious chorus
of the nightingales gathered
from the forest to sing an ode for
Napoleon!

All hail forever!
Yesterday I was an advocate!
Yesterday I was a fool!
Yesterday!

The Beach as a Witness

The beach stood there
and watched
as you hurried there to kill
it saw you pull the trigger
and watch your victims fall
it saw you gather the remains
and throw them in its bosoms

The beach was there
it saw you plunge daggers
deep into your preys
and bury the innocent
in the sand
it saw you running
fleeing from the scenes

The beach was there
it saw you all there
it saw as you dumped
your victims in trucks
and left them there to rot

It saw you take off to your heels
With your masks like a dancer
Fleeing like the cowards, you were

The beach was there
It has answers
for children stolen in its arms
Chained by the waves and
sent to a watery bed

Some had gone for fun
But got nabbed by its gun
The beach was there
When you thought the
world was asleep
The beach saw you
running Hiding under its
shield to wreak your havoc
Someday in court,
you'll see it on the stand
pulling your files before your eyes
The beach is a witness
It was there

Your Country is Mine

I raised my hands in the hallowed hall Swamped by lawyers and judges
And said those words slowly
My lips refusing to move

Scared of the thoughts within
I pledge allegiance to your country
A nation borne for you
Preserved by your forefathers

Here I stand
A total stranger
With my hands lifted
Vowing to preserve your country
A land that was once mine,
My country,
Is no longer mine

Torn from my heart
ripped to shreds
I hold back the tears
and smile at your country

Atlantic waves blow on her
beaches and cool the
residents of Bushrod Island fresh
water flows from
the Kpatawee falls
whilst the Sapo Park
abounds with wildlife

They'll stick as a scar on my mind
as I choose your country over mine
How would your country be mine?
Oh your country is mine

Tanzania Base

Your name sends a chill
Your face sends a silent cold, down
spines, like needles hidden under the
enclaves of CARI, deep in the bosom
of Bong! When men, like chicks, ran
for shelter in your arms, you opened
a door and hid them
under your wings from the gnashing sounds
of gunshots and stray bullets bringing a
relief, life was about to breathe again!

Then, in the darkest of dark,
you pushed us out to the wolves;
shut your huts, took off your
doors, demolished your windows
unmasked your face and, like a
coward, you fled

Oh Tanzania base! Why? You
could have left us alone; let
the lions devour us then.
Or, we would have buried ourselves alive!
But you gave us hope, masked by terror!
And left us out to dry
Wish you'd never been;
wish you were but a dream that would
vanish in the day
Oh Tanzania base,
you broke us like a beast!

Masked In Darkness

*{In memory of the St. Peter's
Lutheran Church massacre}*

It was on a cold, rusty night of July 29
When masked gunmen, stormed your
edifice like butchers set for the
slaughter Why did they prey on babies,
women and children? Were
they afraid to face a battle
as soldiers do? Why wear a
mask in a dark?

Why not face your attackers
the true enemies of the state?
Why prey on the weak?
Do the cries of babies amuse you?
Do their moaning and groaning
Give you strength to bayonet with
your rustic machetes? Did you feel
like a hero?

The night was dark,
as the depth of a rainforest
You marched in as
cowards-Unfit to face
the brow of warfare
You were a dreadful beast

Leave the Line

In those days,
Men dressed like women,
stormed Monrovia
Some wearing wedding
gowns with wigs on their bald
heads like bridesmaids gearing
for a wedding under a downpour
of rain like a flood When men, the
target of mayhem, stood in long
queues
With their wives, children, mothers or sisters
they all feared hearing "Leave the Line!"

Leave the line!
That order meant death back
then When men left those lines,
they were never seen again
Their stories were forever lost,
They vanished into thin air

When I, a child, holding the hand of a
man, desperate for the security it provided
He felt safe with me, a little boy,
for the rebels might not kill him
and leave his boy
He would hold me tight in his hands,
caring for me or himself?

He feared the rebels
could chew him up
what if he didn't
hold a little boy?

When the rebels shouted,
Leave the line!
Men became women,
Shaking like a chicken,
shivering from cold
Their hands hiding behind their backs
their spirits ran before the gunshots
came Men were bundled in cars
tied with their hands behind their backs
like a farmer would bundle his firewood.
The rebels called that 'duck-fat tarbay'
like a duck, tied for slaughter.

Leave the line!
Oh No! That order sent
chills through the spines of men!
When they left the lines,
most of them vanished,
vanished forever!

Midnight in July

*{In memory of the St. Peter's Lutheran
Church Massacre, July 29, 1990}*

*It was midnight, dark, cold
and quiet Fear was alive,
breathing through the pores
of the skies*

*Bam! Bam! Bam!
Went the masked men
with daggers,
spilling blood like rainfall
Cries, echoing deep from their victims,
in disarray rang out like a chorus Let
me live! Let me live! Let me live!
July 29, why did you ever come?*

*It was midnight, in the darkest of the dark
As terror smiled, flexing its fist like an ox
Oh God! They are coming! Help us oh!
Oh God we are dying, where art thou?*

*Tears flowed, like a
riverbank meeting the
ocean's tide terror reigned
killing men & women- even
babies July 29, how did you even
come?*

*'twas a midnight in July,
a longtime ago
But not too long ago
'Tis far away,
but not so far away
The bloody walls
like a slaughterhouse
faint echoes
of gut wrenching screams
of that scary and creepy night*

*Oh July 29,
hope you never
ever come again!*

The Ghost of April 12

Oh April 12! In 1980,
you came many years ago
You took so much- people,
promises, peace, strife- a prize so
grave
Your journey was full of pain,
your flight by mourning,
wrapped with fear
your farewell was abrupt,
mean, embroiled in vengeance
Your tears could fill the ocean-
every drop took its own

When you came, some were dancing,
roaring like caged lions, desperate to
tear apart a lost- vulnerable prey
Some were crying, hiding beneath the
river basin
Others were mourning, grasping for
breath Life was running, leaving, never to
return

Rest in peace April 12, we need you no more;
your memory stings like a scorpion, desperate
for blood and your scars stare at us every day-
guilty of its handiwork
Your imagery smells like a
decomposed carcass-gutted by flies
Hope you're still dead-never to return!

Corruption

The monster we imagine
With horns and claws
that strike like a serpent?
Or with hands as many as
octopus, greedily grasping for
everything? Or, a vampire, sucking
the wealth and lives of nations?

A neighbour, sitting next to us
But slowly draining our veins of its
Blood, as it pulls effortlessly; as creeks
With low tides empty their quotas
into rivers then empty more into the
ocean.

As a toddler, grips his meal in both
hands but, still wanting his mother's
breast milk like a student, on his exams,
gathering answers from left
and right to make an A or a
driver, hiking his fare and
smiling in his heart. Corruption
does not wear a veil It stares at
us everyday
We can wrestle it from the cradle
And then the castle
Corruption is a beast!

Diamonds

Diamonds, oh diamonds,
pretty, shinning, little pebbles
You are precious, meant to
bring relief
to a suffering people

You're holed up in dirt,
lodged safely beneath
the pitch-dark earth,
You're worth millions
that can save a dying nation

But you've brought a curse,
staining hands with blood, you
became blood diamonds

You are a fortune,
draped in splendor;
your glittery sparks the skies
Men from distant lands
troop in numbers
seeking your face
many are lost
in shores way
across the oceans,

You're placed in briefcases,
guided by valiant knights,
escorted by a colorful entourage
You're meant to console
a drowning nation

But you've brought grief,
hands stained with blood, you
became blood diamonds

You are priceless,
pretty; no price tag
can keep you bound
Your face is glittered like a blazing
sun, decked behind a mountain's
face, hidden by the ocean's tide

On diamonds!
You're meant to bless
Poor Africa, but you've brought tears
to home, ravishing her future leaders-
precious jewels, meant for pleasure
but you became blood diamond.

I Wouldn't Be, If You Didn't
(Tribute to my Mother)

If you didn't hold my tiny little fingers
With my hands closed, tightly
around that skinny pencil and shown
me how to trace on a sheet
Perhaps, now, I wouldn't be able to
strike with a pen, like I do now
I wouldn't even be here, writing

If you didn't hold my hands,
during the nasty days of the war,
walking from Matadi to Sawmill,
ICA Camp Sinkor to Duport
Road, walking past dead bodies,
checkpoints manned by bloodthirsty thugs;
I would have been gone-

If you didn't shield my face from them,
so they couldn't hold me up and make me
a small soldier, I would have been lost
to the world of the hopeless, maybe living
on drugs, or left behind, decades back in
everything from ABC to 123

I'm so glad you did, or else
I wouldn't be here, smiling

If you didn't deny yourself food,
when in those days all we had was
palm kernels and sugarcanes
Palm cabbages and wild eddo leaves,
Kissme and cold water fish chased
from the swamps, I wouldn't be alive today,
breathing and still kicking

When food had taken on wheels and ran away
like the ostriches do, when Monrovia had turned
dry, dry like the bottom of a dried out river,
as fish ate fish and crabs ate crabs
You denied yourself food so that
I could eat what little we gathered

If you didn't go out, hiding under stray bullets,
looking for food for us, when all we could look at
was the thick, bare and mean walls, when food
was a luxury, that many could not afford,
I would have probably been left by the
roadside, like many kids were struck to death by
hunger Surely, I wouldn't be here today, living.

Loguato

The tiny, silent village
hidden behind the dark,
vast forest of Nimba
You opened your belly
for many during the conflict
giving them a road to cross
into another land

Upon reaching your gate
Thousands rejoiced
Tears of joy flowed
As people crossed
into another land,
leaving behind their country
and all her woes
Loguato you were a darling,
lending your shoulder to war weary
travelers as they crossed over
They'd come back, someday, maybe.

The African Soldier

The African Soldier
is unpredictable
and does the unthinkable
he's a quiet officer
diligently taking orders
in a fade of minute he's
mean and overzealous,
barking orders everywhere

The African Soldier is desperate
when tamed, he lies before
presidents in prostrate
if not satisfied, he becomes
filled with anger , bringing
terror to the citizens

The African soldier is restless
looking for a fortune
When satisfied, he's like a
hero defending his country
and all other things are a zero

Again?

Are we ready again?
To walk from Matadi to Sawmill?
Jumping over dead bodies,
running through swamps;
chasing Kissmes and Palm Kernels?
Flying from Logan town to Freeport?
Or from Fendell to Kakata?

Are we ready again?
to hang on worn down trucks
Manned by rag tag rebels,
dressed in their wedding gowns,
mimicking a bride who's
awaiting her bridegroom?

Have we heard these words?
In the cause of the people...
There is always a struggle?
To eat, find a shelter,
pay bills, get a life...
Life is more than
ham and cheese,
roads paved with gold
or making a double
There are cracks everywhere,
ruined hopes, tattered dreams,
internal strife; some and more

Beneath those tears,
and dampened spirits,
we should find a truce
In our world, we cheat,
we trick, we hate,
we even bruise...
One quarrel, breeds another,
only a smile can mend a bridge

I, today, don't want to hold
my little girl, running around
in a circle That ends with
another circle, and then
another circle. I no longer
wish to be
waiting for a change,
like a full new moon,
that comes only at night

When my daughter,
grows into a woman and
asks me why I waited
only for the moon and
didn't use the sunlight
to keep life going?
I'd be dumbfounded,
staring the skies for my words

Are They Still Here?

Times have produced men,
sometimes, desperate men
shouting for a change, with a
formula they alone understood
They were the heroes of the people,
pleading a cause in their name
Sending leaders in fear, panicked
and frozen Are they still around?

They were champions of causes
many of their followers did not see
Bu they, with ideas years ahead,
Forged along beyond the hills
forward with their firebrand fists,
their youthful vibrancy,
they broke down mountains
with little else but effort and
great perseverance

They were the warriors that men knew,
they were the gladiators of then
The people, like cheerleaders,
gave them their backs to blow
things over
Are they still here?

Sometimes, I wonder,
are these men still around?
Most of them are,
sitting quietly at the table
With their heads bowed,
ignoring the people,
they once stood for

They've arrived and
are now seated
At the emperor's table.
They partake,
Of the feast…
dining with royalties

Oh fate where are thou?
See your boys that roared
with fire
in the 70's, 80's and 90's
Time is deceptive,
leaving itself only to memories
The ghost of leaders, deposed,
can only stand still and linger.

God Bless You?

I reached this point they call
It "God bless you gate"
Oh God! Why don't I feel blessed?
I'm faced with beasts
Why do savages reign here?
And say your name in vain?
God bless them!

When I fled the flames
I came to the line
I thought was the finished line
A wig-wearing child looked at me
And with a sigh he said
Welcome to the last gate
Put your hands in the air
This is the 'God bless you gate'

September 9

The walls crumbled
They caught a man
A Country's flag bearer
Chaos winked at the drugged gangs
Barking orders
Mocking their prey
Hands fastened to the back...
How did we reach here?

You took away a boot
One of the 17 boots
You took the camouflage too,
You wrote history with the blood of innocents
Were you on a revenge for April 12? Maybe?

G2

I remember your name
I still do
"G2"! Shouts a rag tag officer
Put him in there
In the G2
The home of torture

Where are you now?
G2 shouts a rag tag officer
Leave your rights behind
Here, we own you,
Forgot where you are?
This is the G2!

Freedom Fighter

You're a slave
To those that feed you
With crack and coke
Poor child,
You ain't no Freedom Fighter
Go home and take a bath
Remove the veil and wigs

Freedom fighter
Oh boy!
I once longed for you
Do you kill to free us
of our miseries?
Do you maim and rape?
To free us of our destitute
I'd rather be a prisoner 'cuz
I don't need a freedom fighter

14 Road

You greeted us with darkness
You exposed our bags to thugs
Everything we had we gave
Money, slippers, soap
Even our voices
14 road
I can only sigh

You were helpless
As kids ruined your town
Turning men to babies
All you did was stare
Who could dare
When parents lay down
Their lives to save their families?

Wigs of Terror

They came wearing wigs
like mamas and her friends wore
they came as men in wedding gowns
branding guns
machetes and knives

but their knives didn't cut fish to cook
they drove into us like chickens I
don't fear mama
But, they're not my mama
They're freedom fighters
They're bandits…

They wore wigs
dressed in wedding gowns
though the occasion
was not festive
they were living nightmares
fixing to take us captive

Flames in the Air

tires burning,
with litters trooping upwards
in a pattern of fear
a nation rips itself apart
as tears pour down
on the swollen faces of children,
parents face the interrogators,
the elderly or sick lie
in wheelbarrow helpless
where have we come?
the flames burn a generation...

everything was burning,
written in flames
millions of stories burned to ashes
as memories of pain untamed
join the circle of smoke
the flames told stories of a
nation that had committed
arson where are the culprits?

they are coming

crowds rushed with bundles of
clothes, chicken, everything
their faces told it all
'they are coming'
no further questions
needed to be asked
the marathon began
we all just keep going
they are just coming…

they are coming!
bring the babies
take our mattresses
bring the chickens
and the goats too,
tell no one my name
not even the neighbors
for none is a brother
no one knows
they are coming!

who born soldier

the chanting roared
with cheers of unknown heroes
the soldiers had come the
hideouts are broken
'who born soldier?'
who knows

one mother cries,
another mother weeps
now, both mothers cry
'who born soldier'
no one knows
now, the nation weeps

who born soldier?
who born soldier?
remember those lines
those chants?
still want to jubilate
or to chant again?

What's Your Tribe?

Sixteen brothers live here
all of different names
Why do you hunt me?
My tribe scares you?
Why so? Don't be
We're parts of a whole
Same blood, one people

Come over here
What's your tribe
I could feel my spirit
Jump out on a flight
My lips abandoned
my tongue stuck
as it tried to speak

17 boots

17 scary boots
all midnight hovers
scaring crickets
dragging out their preys

Mask wearing scarecrows
turned the dagger on others
slaying by day and night
17 scary boots imprint themselves

Bloody footprints

of your time here we see
Where art thou now
17 scary boots?

Caldwell

Got a story of soldiers
and rebels standing over
their weakened prey
hands tied to his back

Duck-fat tie-bay victim
pleading for his life
offering everything
life ever bestowed
to his captors

Got a story of a tyrant
now begging drunken
soldiers Boom! Boom! Boom!
one more booth down
poor soldier who killeth thou?

Palm Cabbage

A lifesaver
During the war
A household darling in the pots
Every home could court
A stitch in time
The palm tree gave itself away
The kernels
The cabbage
Even the branches kept a home

Carter's Camp

You were asleep
They crept on you
And broke your walls
And stole your cattle
Butchered your sons
Raped your daughters
Stole your peacefulness
In all this horror
you were helpless
Watched them change shifts
In destroying your peace
They killed the silence
That blessed you at night
And they were mostly babies
Why did men fear babies?

Memories of a Lonely Prisoner

She sits alone
Thoughts pouring
through her arteries
she makes a note
to flyaway someday
leaving her captors
find the rustic chains
or checking the walls
for her shadows; only to wonder
if the girl there had balls
To break the iron framed cage

Freedom was a breath away
She knew this in her soul
Not even the gates of a prison cell
Could lock the power of her mind

Nov 2

The dudubors came
With wings that spilled
bullets wherever they could
it burned down people,
places the bush and flowers;
anything
The sound left men stunned
in silence
Afraid to hold their babies
Forced men to scurry like
ants Oh Nov 2!
You left a stain
Come and clean your mess
And hush the voices you left in
tears It's your handiwork
Even time can't free you

Jungle Warriors

Warriors of the desolate
Or for shoes and
Wristwatches?
Afraid of the jungle
Your home?
Jungle warriors
Or city cowards?

Totota

Come here, girl
Proud sister
Your shield was strong
Blinded from thugs and bandits
You kept a treasure
Of fleeing people
Come here girl
Take your medal
This is your time
Thank you, Totota

The White Helmet Shot My Brother

They came
Dressed like angels
We raised our hands
In the air like kites
They cut our nightmares
We fled to meet our friends
Leaving behind memories
Of drugged teenagers
With hurried steps we came

Bam, bam, bam!
Went the shots
Into a promise of tomorrow
They broke up his uncovered years
With hopes of generations
A moment of indiscretion
Shattered a promise
Did the white helmet fear his innocence
Could break his riffle to pieces?
Or his bare chest would melt bullets
Like a goldsmith?
A coward stood under the helmet
Barricaded by fear.

Sept 23

they came at night
gathering and holing us like cattle
we were led by their AK 47s
doctors and nurses were the prey
Phebe was the butcher's camp
Jungle Warriors,
Bandits,
ULIMO,
each taking turns
The ground bear us witness
the walls could not empty
the wailing of voices captured
from the echoes of cries

Smokes in Gbarnga

Gbarnga,
dear magnificent Gbarnga a
city for the poor and rich now
dancing with the warriors
Poor child,
You had no choice
They lit you in flames
when done
they scrambled
over your ruins

Trek to Ganta

Oh Ganta
You embodied hope
To fainthearted
Civilians
Fleeing carnage arms
When Gbarnga fell
You stood up
with open arms
We still remember you

Kokoya Road

Hey there,
I know you were there
You saw horrors of
Men slain
On your paths
Dogs and maggots
Gathered their debris
You saw all that
And more, now
Free your soul, for
Today is a better day

Mae Davis

Let tomorrow one day
Read a diary of you
Of the space you gave
To children
Of the cornmeal you served
To grateful tiny fingers
Of the big hands
You covered their faces
With protecting them
From the fire piercing eyes of
Warriors hunting for recruits
Thank you

The Peacekeeper

I saw a peacekeeper
Who signed deals with barbarians
And gave gasoline to thugs
And went looking for water
Watching his deeds from up
On the small window
Of my grandmother's hut

I saw a peacekeeper
Steal my sister's hands
And broke my brother's arms
Why did you come here,
Peacekeeper?
To laugh with our captors
And enslave our girls?
A hero at day,
A heathen by night

He was Dancing

We put on the television
And saw your father dancing
Happy for the capture of today

My father pulled his
machete And went hunting
Brought your father's head home

He was dancing
I never understood why
Not even today

April 6

What happened?
A drug deal gone bad
Or a cartel gone rogue
Barbarians against barbarians
What really happened
We were pawns that
Even ships refused us
Countries looked away
High waters awaited our
bodies Streetfighters and
cannibals brought Monrovia to
her knees No it wasn't April's
fool, son, Remember April?
14 or April 12?
Not April's fault boy
Just men chasing clouds

Bulk Challenge

A stitch in time
that burst
in the middle of night
stowaways and runaways
mingled
even money didn't matter
big shots and gronaboys
ate together
overnight friends
emerged on
Bulk Challenge

I have Worn Scars

When I tell the world
that I bore a scar for ages
they sigh in doubts
Cuz my smile give
an illusion of how
blur the physical lends itself
I've seen wounds smile
when pierced,
cuz they carry unblemished
strength that have survived age old
bruises Someday
when this story is written,
the author's script
would borrow
from the leftover smiles.

Note

The next set of poems are not war poems but are included because they form part of our collective history of pain and sorry as a nation. These Ebola pieces touch a small but significant point in the life of a nation that had to face a new type of war. This one was not with bullets, knives, and machetes but from a deadly disease.

The devastation of Ebola was enormous but the resolve of Liberians proved stronger and potent enough to beat it back on several occasions.

This is a Liberian horror story as well. In some ways, it was war in its own rights. We lost many battles, won some here and there and struggled to overcome, but overcome we did. We won this war as a people. We won by dropping our political and social divides and taking this disease head on regardless the costs.

When Ebola Hits Home

How do you run
when a mobster hits your door
and puts your kids at gunpoint
shaking them in fear Do you
hide your face
and pray he flees?

Where do you hide
when a serial killer slits
the throat of your mother?
Do you stand and watch her
bleed to death?
Or call the cops or ambulance?
Would you fold your arms
and turn the corner?

When do you act when
your child is gasping for breath?
After the last air evaporates?
Scared to death that yours is next
Are you a coward, a villain or hero?

When Ebola hits home
courage turns cold
Chained by fear, horror and
fate Do I walk, run or watch and
see my brother, my granny or sister

Burn to death by vampires of flesh?
The serial killer preys on blood
He marvels at it and strangles to death
Looking around for a next victim

Ebola at home is as deadly
as a forest fire
Just one torch ignites again
Who is this forgotten killer?
You're not fit to carry a
name But borrows one after
a river somewhere Die
forever, Ebola

A Liberian, not Ebola
(*Inspired by the campaign against stigmatization*)

I am a Liberian, not some virus
red blood flows through my veins
My heart beats like hydro,
pumping through those arteries I
am human, not a parasite
I live on rice, fish and meat,
not on blood and carcass

I got brains, I'm not dumb

I am alive as a bird,
chirping on trees
enjoying nature
I'm not a night walking
fanged vampire
drinking the red life
out of people
nor am I a leech
sucking people's blood
Ebola does not
live here
How then can I be
the virus Ebola?

Check the St. John River
the Cavalla River
Or from St. Paul's
To the Gbelleh forest,
Go up the Wologisi Mountain
It's nowhere here child
How do I own this thug?

My country is rich with green rainforests
A wonderful climate and beautiful history
Amazing culture and Africa's first child

Do we have labs
that make malaria?
How could we be Ebola?
I am a Liberian
From the land of the free
I am a Liberian,
a warm blooded mammal;
a human, an African
a Homo sapiens,
not a virus!

Ebola, Go Away

Your time is up!
You're a stranger, an enemy
Leave this space and go away

Your venom has struck
Bringing down pillars, built over years
Tearing apart men and women of valor
Ever digging beneath the depths of pain

But, where is your strength? To
rip to shreds the flesh that
even a spin can send to rest?

Can you break the strength of united hearts?
Or bruise the will of a silent hero?
No, no you're just another thug roaming
aimlessly like an armed bandit

You're a loser; a lone traveller Lost
in the tropical rainforest Get out of
here and go away! Run back to
where you originated! what is your
name? Ebola?
You don't even have a name
You're remembered after some river
Cuz, no one even cared about you

Leave the corridors of Foya
Market And vanish from the slums
of West Point and Waterside
You chose the wrong target
A people whose courage
is harder than the hardest steel
stronger than a camel's back but
with strength to blow away your venom

Lost in our resolve as a people Shot in
the legs by our patriotism We booted
out the evil virus Your mission has
failed, go away Your target was
missed, go away Those you took are
smiling from above, resting in peace

You took them to a better place,
go away Ebola

Go to the belly of tiny fruit bats
And slam your face in shame,
beating yourself with hate
'21days' is your strength of
time And we live on forever
Ebola, go away.

Blocked Gates

In the quarantine space the
gates are blocked Walls are
jammed with men Longingly
staring at freedom Like
caged animals they gasp
for air
Hoping some relief
could spill from above

Suspicion roams
the doors are shut
Knob knitted tightly
locked with fear
Scared of themselves
everything is a farce
Their homes are silent,
wearied to hold them

Even mothers are afraid of
babies Husbands shun their wives
The new girl-Ebola sparks fear
Her spirit rules the time

Barbed wires hold the keys
Manning the gates with a fierce face
Y'all dare not cross or meet your fate
The stabber smiles at his shallow preys

In those blocked gates
Occupants are contained
Like the living from the dead
And the living from the ready to die

The young, the old, the weak, the strong
The rich, the poor, the meek the great
All hurdle with one space
Forced to have a voice

Fate turns the arms of time
Spinning foes into friends
The strike of a mutual enemy forges unity
With no sweat, no true, neither a dime

When Ebola Leaves

I can feel the day deep within my soul
When we can shake hands again
And embrace without fear
When boys and girls can walk to school
And play like birds soaring on skies

I can see the smiles
on the faces of teachers as
they hug their students glad
to give them knowledge

I can smell the palm butter
and smoked fish being steamed from
the cookshops and restaurants

I can hear the horns of pehn pehn boys
Blaring like bats on top of the world
I can feel the breadth of the preacher man thanking
God for answered prayers

I can see the sun smiling greetings at us
with hope from above when Ebola leaves
We would all be merry keep those little buckets
manning the doors like a baby left by Ebola

Screams from the ETU

I heard a shout
Soaring in the night
Held by the echoes
Then a sob
Drippling tears
Faced with cockroaches
and crickets
The flying breeze
of mosquitoes
Tickling my ears
I skimmed the rooms
Scary tears
The space suit attendants
Peeping at me
Where is this?
Border of death?
The screams were short
Scary to the soul
Chocked by fear
Even water is priceless
Hell might be a better place.

PART 2

Exile Screams

*Mothers try to hush
Voices of babies soaring
Echoes choke the night*

Danane!

Danane! Oh Danane!
I remember you with smiles and tears
Your arms securely held us- desperate,
frightened people, fleeing for our lives

When we crossed that small timber bridge
and saw your dusty face from afar,
we breathed a sigh of life
Our hearts jumped with
joy, oh what a day!

In a new land Danane- uncertainty
dominated our emotions.
Now away from the dangers of war,
we braced to face
the new challenges of this land
Oh, Danane was that place!

At times, you were just so mean
sometimes so cruel;
your scorching sun rained on our tiny
refugee zinc top roofs like ice drops,
tin, tin, tin,
plop, plop plop,
your rain blazed
flowing as a flood

Oh Danane, where is your arrogance?
Why did you keep us under the
Sun and Rain at Nyenglay,
at the distribution site,
waiting for rice and burger wheat,
Or vegetable Oil and cornmeal?

From Petit Danane to La Gare de
Man, from Belleville to Houphetville,
even all the way
from Air France to Beer Garden
you covered us deeply in your
wings We could ride your white taxi
cabs, or walk in group to school,
chatting, fondly for a better life

On Sundays, oh mine!
The Churches would be full, Liberians, on yes!
You'll see them dancing in Churches and
waiting to someday comeback home
or join the resettlement train, off to America!

Danane, where are our
children? You took so much with
you, buried deep in your bosom,
Danane! Oh Danane!
We miss you but with tears and fears,
our hearts are full of your memories!

Landlord

During my refugee days in Danane
My landlord would creep over my
roof to make sure I didn't pierce it
with my evening singing
he would wake up in the morning,
exploring the yard like a tourist;
inspecting the ground my children played on,
the paint on my tiny *chambre et salon**;
He would jump in my kitchen
desperate to see the food I cooked
His eyes would shine like a fluorescent bulb,
wanting to see if I bought chicken, *bonny*
or spare ribs. He'd want to see
If I bought cow meat, and if I did, oh no!
I'll be in trouble
how could I, a refugee, eat cow? My
landlord was an unwanted visitor Running
in my living room like a new suitor anxious
to please his young new bride His face
was always full of pride
My landlord became a nightmare
Roaming my world with an uneasy stare

* *French- for one bedroom and living room attached.*

La Marie

Open your chest
Show us the voices you caged
Of lads giggling at talent shows
Pin our ears to the melody of choirs
That left voices there from concerts
And bring alive lost souls

Play recordings of the
Cherubims,
Seraphims,
the Revelators...
And let today bow in awe
of the memories of time
Flown away forever

If I Went Back Today

If I went back to Danane' today,
would memories be all that I see?

If I went back to La Marie, would I
see the beautiful choirs geared
up in their beautiful colors, like the
lilies of the valley?
Or would I only hear echoes of their melodies,
ringing from afar deeply lost in my memories?
Would I ever see them there?

If I went to the Futu shops
I would only stand and weep
cuz I'll be thinking of the
days when us boys would
gang up and eat like hungry
warriors-just from a battle.

If I went back to Nyenglee and
stood at the site of the distribution
center I would get lost,
far in my thoughts, would I feel the weight
of the burger wheat on my head as I ran
like a speedboat to my house?

If I went to St. Jeans or PMRC and
sat and stared, my oh my! Would I
cry or smile as I see images of boys
and girls in white and green, of lads
sitting and chatting
I'd never see those guys we sat
with, ate and even fussed.

If I went to CEG or customs field, where
St. Jeans and St. Martins met or PMRC
and Mountain View clashed or MERCY
and Union Baptist battled where the
soccer matches of the titans took
place, would I still feel the rush? I'd get
lost in the past

If I went back to the bus station at CTDD,
CTM, Nimba Voyage or Cavalla Voyage,
would I still see my friends boarding for
Abidjan? Would time and fate be fair?
If I went to Hotel Leon or Hotel Tia, went
to the Maquis or L'espoire, will I be alone?
If I watched 'faux pas factuher'* on
Saturday would I be lonely in my world? If I
ever went back, would memories haunt me?

* A local sitcom...

Nimba Voyage

the bullet train with tires
taking men to abidjan
the big city, to jam
with televisions on board
leaving refugees in awe
nimba voyage
i remember that name
some memories stain...

The Telephone booth

People gathered
On a refugee camp
They formed lines
To dial the lines
Of a friend, relative
anyone who'd answer
To lend a hand
In a dismal situation
The camps were dire
Anything could help
Even a promise
that never came

somedays, men walked away,
broken, but always came back

Men gathered and lectured
Kept old memories alive
Like a palm wine tree
The telephone booths
were there
Keeping souls alive

Put My Number In

my number
just slide it in
someone might hear
and call back
thus offering
my only hope
of another day
something to hold on to
even straws that sink
any hope could inspire

The Resettlement Interview

everyone gathered
for the day
the family assembled
even strangers made the roll
looking forward to the day
of the promised land
do you remember your name?
how could I not, mother?
the place we live?
desperation looms
like a ticket on titanic
it's no turning back
judgement day in exile
came on that day

Distribution Site

I remember
The queues
The burger wheat
The Argo oil
The sweet chatters while
waiting For something to hold
Cornmeal, biscuit,
Anything could do
I miss those day, sometimes

PMRC

The hut that kept scholars
hungry to feed off the fountain
of men and women who gave freely

From Moribadougou to Belleview
Houphetville to La Gare de Man
Nyenglay to Liberia road
came sons and daughters who
yearned for the depth of knowledge

Meet the challenge and
debate they were the titans
a cradle of academic excellence
now all flown to distant lands
but the memories cuddle in their
hearts Where are they now?

PART 3

Stolen Innocence

*Babies became men
Families stretched in thin shreds
Drugs and crime reign here*

They Took My Daughter

Men came to our house
Where is she, they roared!
My heart leapt from my chest
My soul wept for her
My pearl of only 11 years
Oh god! Blind the eyes of these killers
I can't lose her
No not now
Spare me Lorpu,
Spare me Sabah, Miriam,
Kou, Korto, Juah
Leave my daughter
In broken tears,
I hushed,
I flared my hands
angrily in air
Why now?
Oh Helen, Nenjay,
Ade, Fatumata,
Please bring her back
I waited….
I'm still waiting.

Double-Edged

I felt it travel down my spine
And loosened a chill that squeezed
my nerves into submission
Iron fisted arms beat my hands
to the ground where my back
was fastened to the earth

My eyes swelled in tears
as the double edge slit my pie. In
my daydream voices struggled
for a grasp of air. I was hallucinating on my
surgical bed manned by my captors
A captive of culture?

The drips found their way between
my towers that failed themselves.
Crushed to pick my gold
between, they dug out my
treasure But my soul remained
my voice too remained
It's buried beyond their reach
They forgot that I'm a goldmine.

Broken Rose

they plucked her pie
uprooted her diamond
tree she kept for a prize
pulled violently by thugs
enslaved by cracks they
broke her rose
her golden bulb
and left her bruised
and bleeding

Marriage at Twilight

They came
We became cooks
They broke our men
We became wives

All this happened
At twilight…

I Wanted to Be

I wanted to be...
a doctor was my dream
a teacher my brother's
a mechanic my cousin's
a pilot my sister's
but they came and with
their gifts of guns and drugs
we became what they made us
night peddlers
midnight roamers
car loaders
now,
we're the terror of the state
we just wanted to be...

My Brother Died Living

My brother died
Of hope, vibrancy and zest
he wanted to become everything
But given bread of crack,
coke and guns
he left ahead a fortune
And abandoned life forever
Living in shacks and ghettos
While he felt like a king
Cuz drug had made him think so
My brother was long dead
While living...

Massaquoi-taa

Massaquoi-taa, your name
rings like an old school bell
When I hear of you, I think of
years, way, way back
When your face was innocent,
calm, like a virgin's brow,
Children like me, then,
could not say a curse around you, for
fear of the unknown, or the elders
would roar like a thunder that vibrates
like an explosion
When vacation came in December,
oh yea, we'd be sitting in the moonlight,
watching the dancers shake their bodies
like a rooster does, smelling the breeze
of Christmas, filling the air with dust, and
watching it rise slowly to the sky and
disappear.

Oh Massaquoi-taa, where is your
patience? When Monrovia was
burning, we would run to your
bosom, hiding our face behind
your back, decked under your
feathers,
we felt safe under those shadows,
barricaded from the scars of war

But the war did tear you up Massaquoi
ta; it took away your innocence,
your demeanor and elegance,
once firmed like a brick wall- reassuring.
It took away your benevolence that
kept its entire heritage, firmly in one bundle.
It ripped you of your pride, left crumbled
and neglected, deprived of your beauty.

That aura that once abided,
creating a magnet with your off springs,
was washed away, along the river's bank.

Oh Massaquoi-taa, where is your touch?
Massaquoi-taa, land of my mother's birth, there
I could walk and smile, sitting on my
grandmother's lap, as she rolled her basket,
ready for fishing. My sisters and me, would run in
the hood, chasing grasshoppers we call Jack,
or we'd run away from the sounds
of birds and Sembe- tu-tu

At night, we'd cry from the sounds of frogs, crying
in on chorus, chanting like an orchestra On the
outskirts of Margibi, this small little village, found
along the bolo-la river is Massaquoi-taa!

You Dumped Us

you armed us
in our teens
gave us crack
to stir our brains
then left with machetes
to bring your loot

we were your Guinea pigs
doing your biddings
as you smiled
and hid your face
Brought your medals in absentia
Cowards of fame

we were the blacksmiths that
molded and gave you shapes
now that you're formed
you send us back to our cages
you told them to call us Zokos
we might meet again, Nokos

Small Soldier

Small Soldier
Not so small
With an evil filled heart
huge as a mountain
you were merciless and brutal
You were a villain,

Small soldier, poor soldier
Hooked to drugs and powder
Led like a slave to kill and maim
You outperformed your ruthless tasks

With calm restored after the chaos
Poor soldier, recruited by force
Scared of the society you destroyed
Stolen innocence, small soldier

Cry for them small soldier
Simple mind, packed with crack
Poor child, surrogate killer
Small soldier, I cry for you

He's Only 5

Poor baby
only five
holding an AK 47
Taller than his tiny frame
Now a serial killer
What happened?

PART 4

Hope for the Future

*Light shines in the doom
Capturing the lens ahead
Of hope eternal*

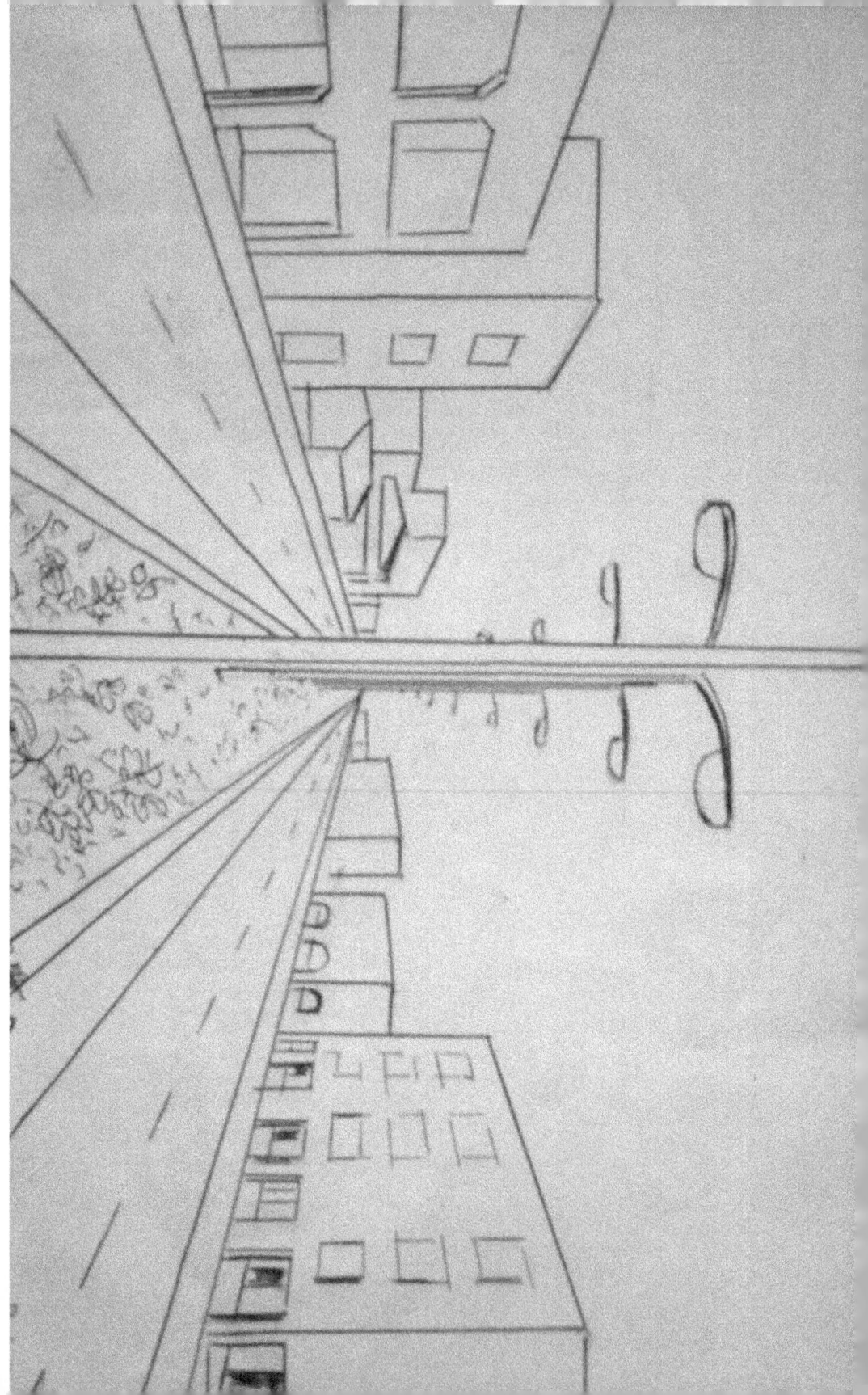

When the Ancestors Return

When our Ancestors return
what would they see?
Ruins of a city they
labored to build?
And remnants of tools
they dared to keep?
Would they love to see a treasure
blown away by the breeze?
They might just stand afar and weep

When they ask of the gold
and diamond
What would we say-
we gave them up for
peanuts and live in destitute?
When we see their faces-
would we see dismay?

Oh child, let's get to work
Our ancestors might soon be here
Or we might flee, burdened with shame.

Africa, the hour is here
Get on board and make it work

On the Back of History
(For Liberia)

On the back of history
Came a small colony
A home of the Negroes
A land for them to smile
The first little country
In the breast of Africa
On the back of history
came men and women
spurred by will and valor,
one people united in adversity
when bullied by the bulldozers They
stood strong, arms under arms, and
declared a free nation

On the back of history, came Maryland,
creeping, crawling, crying to join her
brothers and sisters in love as a nation

On the back of history
came men and women of color
Roaming Africa for a land to rest
and to live and to call home.
They came from distant kingdoms
Some from Ancient Ghana, Mali, or
the Songhay empire
These daughters and sons of traders,
came in search of a place to call home

On the back of history
came the sons of King Sao Boso,
King Long Peter; the sons of Bob Gray;
the sons of Matilda Newport
sailing on the back of history on the
Mayflower, Elisabeth, Alligator, Cora
Our ancestors dreamed that one day,
their children would sit down together
void of tribe or ethnicity and write the stories
of their fathers with a lens clearer than any
binoculars for our country is a tye-dye nation

All sixteen tribes came with one voice
From cape Mesurado, to Bushrod Island
From Lofa to Nimba; Bong to Grand Cape
Mount; From Grand Gedeh to Grand Bassa;
someday, we'll see the faces of our neighbors
trooping to our land. This time, not for slaves,
but to see the shores of Bushrod Island
where the men of color lived; or see the shores
of Lake Piso; or wander behind the forest of the
Sapo Park; or picnic on the sides of Kpatawee,
all along the mangrove swamps;
and tropical rainforests
Then, we will ring the bell of our chorus
The love of Liberty
Brought us here!

Vision 2030

Liberia has a vision...
Seen afar in 2030
there will be
roads, schools, hospitals...
all in 2030.
A dream carried for ages
We harbor a mission

Liberia rising out
of the dungeon,
of the ugly past with a new fashion
Come on board, every Liberian
from Bong to Lofa,
Nimba to Grand Gedeh, Sinoe
to Maryland all Liberians who
have the passion
This is the hope beyond the mansion
It'll be hard with no cushion but
we'll meet there in unison

As Liberians sit and meet
in every county, clan,
village or town in a working
session The vision for Liberia
will become
One day it will hatch
with every Liberian
a part of the decision

the days are gone
for fighting,
tearing and pulling-
every Liberian will get his
ration Speak for views
with no tension.

Gbarnga Again!

A long, time ago
Piles of dust shot the skies, as
people cramped to sign a
nation's lease in Gbarnga

Gbarnga held the feet of men and
cars as voices defied the
deafening silence of a calm city
whilst men adopted a constitution

In 1994 everything went south
A once vibrant city, a cradle of hope
Grew cold and shivered in fear and
watched helplessly as strangers sprayed
gunshots and pierced its wonderful skin
Gbarnga came crumbling-

Will Gbarnga rise again?
Wondered an elder as he
reminisce on its glory days

Oh Gbarnga, someday,
You shall rise again to glory
One day soon, Gbarnga will smile
Soon the great city shall wake.

Cars descend once again
on Gbarnga this time,
not to shoot, and loot
they gathered afar on a hill,
smiling at the future;
deciding the fate
of a new nation
In Gbarnga again!

You are Lifted!

You are lifted!
Your face shines above the axis
Suffering and calamity now bow
Flush out your worries
in the depth of the ocean

You're lifted
oh land of my nativity-
come into my arms,
your name imprinted by time
price paid by stripes of blood
Foes faint at thy moment
None can hurt you anymore,
My country is lifted 'neath the dirt
our flag soar like a kite
we cherish thy memory
Our souls are lifted!

Lift Liberia

Lift Liberia! Lift Liberia!
Together, with hands united,
lets' take Liberia from the cliff
Come every Liberian;
from the unforgotten slums
Swamps and ghettoes let her not drift If
Liberia is lifted, our hearts shall be kind

Lift Liberia! Lift Liberia!
Bring your questions, ideas and time
Let's sit in groups and decide the
future of our own beloved Liberia
If Liberia is lifted, peace our minds shall find

Lift Liberia! Lift Liberia!
Come on Elders, youth and all Bring
your wisdom, energy and zest-let's
rebuild our shattered motherland If
Liberia is lifted, our nation shall bind

Promise

I am the heart, the hope of the state!
The fulfillment of yesterday to date!
I am the pride and the promise,

That needs the time and the space to beam!

Please dear elders don't make me to burn!
For this country, depends on me in-turn!
I am the dream and hope of tomorrow!
Oh dear elders, don't fill me with sorrow!

For years I've known
nothing but trouble!

Now is the time
for me to double!

I am the life and promise of Liberia;
The one who'd raise it in honor!

Oh elders I can never
be your tool in terror!

My Country is Mine!

My country is mine
A land of my nativity
many years before
My ancestors kept it with their
Tears, sweat and blood
and died to preserve this land

is Liberia still

a land of the free?
My resting place
The corner I call home
Its roads could be broken,
with potholes as deep as
cooking pots or fire hearth
But I love my country

With hands joined, over time
Liberia shall smile broadly and
shine like the face of mercury
I love thee Liberia My country
is mine!

My Country, Your Country, 1 Country!

A place the wind blows slowly,
A land left behind by our ancestors A
country with two beautiful seasons This
is our land- my country, your country
When the rain falls, covering the roads
like a flood, leaving behind its debris
Littered on the surface like dead bugs,
helpless, and horrible
Kids filled with joy and laughter
jump under its shadows, to get a
bath, Bathing under the rain, running
in pairs like birds do

This is our heritage-
my country, your country
In the dry season, it's hot like the face of
the planet Mercury
The earth is dry and scotching as the top of a
bare concrete roof-top. Our tribes came crashing
from afar- all strangers, rested on this land
Today, we are all mixed up like Jollof rice,
 my tribe, your tribe, your name, my name
This is our home,
my country, your country

One Race, One Blood One Liberia

Oh children, you are one race, one
blood all one people- Liberians You
all came from distant lands and
found this country...
We are all Liberians

Fate took some in chains
to foreign plantations working hard,
building the lands of strangers all Liberians;
others remained here keeping the country,
its heritage left by our ancestors, our
common patrimony.
We are all Liberians.

Oh children, one history,
one culture, one Koloqua,
all Liberians
After years of segregation,
some on foreign
plantations others here,
you had a family reunion,
first in 1822...
all Liberians.

Over time, we fought,
opinions divided us; passion
separated us but, bound by
history and heritage let's join
hands
in union strong
our success is sure.
Let's keep our lands and
build a better nation
Oh children, one family,
one country,
Know that
we are all Liberians.

I Found My Compass

I paced around the corner; lost in my
tracks The roads seemed blurred; eyes
were shut to the possibilities that abounded
I was stuck in grief, in mediocrity The
journey was vague and endless
Then I found a flash of light that
penetrated deep in the pores of the forest
I looked above the beams
And flew towards my dream
I found my path-stored in the lead of a pencil.
I broke the shackles of Illiteracy with the pen
between my fingers; I found my compass
buried in the pages of a book
I leapt from the wings of captivity
Manned by the fear
Of teenage pregnancy
Of rape
Of domestic violence
Of marginalization
Of one million voices telling me to stop
I paused and listened to a lone voice
that told me I could soar Beyond my
bondage stood a world, willing to
embrace me
I found my compass and,
I became...

I Celebrate a Soldier

I celebrate a Soldier
Today, I celebrate a Soldier
the one that died on frontlines
defending this land I call home
the one whose bloodstains
remain on the bank of the St. John's

I celebrate a soldier-
not the one that buried babies alive
and ate the hearts of the innocent

I celebrate a soldier
that fought by his oath
to rescue a nation
we hold dear today
Not the gangs that marched
in churches and slayed
citizens with machetes like
butchers. May their memories
fade with the ocean's tides.

I celebrate a soldier,
a patriot, a hero.
Not a murderer, a vampire,
a death squad coward,
a midnight bandit.
I celebrate a Soldier!

Unification Time

Holding hands from the
back of Wologisi in Lofa to
Bomi From the bosom of
Lake Piso in Cape Mount to
Rivercess and Gbarpolu to
Bong,
on the shoulders of Kpatawee,
to the eyes of the Nimba forest
It's Unification time!

Come out!
Hold our hands,
up in the air and
shout one chorus!
We are one!
Let's unite!

Red, White and Blue

On a cold, quiet day
sometime in August,
a cloth was woven into a flag
From a simple cotton thread in a
cloth, a national symbol lay bare,
exposed for all to see
24 August, rainy, cold and calm,
Liberia became gay

Eleven stripes, rolled beautifully,
hoisted above the fray they
were red, white
and blue- not gray
Not all colors stood with us,
With a modest will,
sat Susannah Lewis and
her team of seven, all women,
strong, brave and gallantly
toiling the night away; toiling
the time with no pay

Red, white and blue, red, white and blue!
These colors held together, to bind us like glue!
Other nations will watch our bond without a clue!
With bravery, valor and purity, our country
is out of the blue!

Let's Forget [Reconciliation Poem]

Oh Liberians!
Oh Liberians!
Let's forget!
But please do not neglect
The dreams of our fathers
and hopes of our children to beget
Those dreams and hopes we
fought for with tears
We should always protect
and defend with no fears.

From Cape Montserrado to Cape Palmas
from Wologisi to Cestos, let us embrace
our brothers, sisters, fathers, uncles,
aunties, nephews and all with grace
the oceans, rivers, lakes, villages,
clans, towns are ours
The green forest, trees, hills, mountains...
this glorious land of liberty shall long
remain ours

Oh Liberia!
Land of one race,
creed, people, culture,
destiny and one color
We shall forever march
and hold this nation
with great Valor

Great nation,
home of the homeless,
land of the free
You shall forever hold
this family together
under one tree

Oh Liberians!
Oh Liberians!
Let's reconcile
For this land is our domicile!

Tribute Pieces

Thank you Yah (To be read in Kpelleh)

(In loving memory of my grandmother)

Yah, thank you,
where ever you are
I hope you are fine,
let God be with you
Your children say hello oh
Your oldman is a young man now
Your husband says hello
Lekpele is a big man now;
his arms are wide as a big cotton
tree Guladia is a young girl too She
even has a baby
Your other oldman Demoi
is now a young man oh
Even Belala has a child

Can you See Nowai and the others?
Please say hello to them
Say hello to Lucky too,
Tell her we miss her yah
Please say hello to aunty Nowai,
Tell her the children say hello yah

Can you see Peter too?
Tell him longtime yah,
Tell him the children are big,
big now yah
Eh yah, when we think about you,
sorrow can catch our arms like a whirlwind
Holding us tight with a grip
Tunpau, Big brother Musa and Ab,
all say hello yah
When you see Nyamalon,
tell him hello yaa
Me, Belekula,
I can really miss you
Yah God bless you
Until we meet again
Ah yah, tears,
ahhh my people
Aaaaa yahhhh!

Tribute to all those who Died During the Civil Conflict

A brother
A sister
One woman's only child
On a rampage down Camp
Johnson Road Gunned
down by stray bullet Inspired
by the foot soldiers of a
promise
To bring down the price of
rice A family cried alone
As the trumpet voices hung in the
air And dined with the butchers
While the masses lingered

I saw your son down Carey Street
Stuck between broken glasses
and Left the TV set staring at him
Life took flight that day
17 best friends fought over a
pie And spilled acid on the
faces of each other
As a revolution went rogue
And elections manned by the
barrel of the gun Dropped
from coveted hands And
broke in pieces

While the debris choked
a nation in trauma
Revolution part 2
Took us on a journey
With rag tag boys in wigs
Living on weeds
Tearing the curtains that covered our
faces And the world rushed and saw the
scars we had hidden for ages
The cracks in the walls broadened
as each brick let loose by time Fell
over us and broke the bonds that
kept us going

Mothers gang raped and beaten
Fathers made to crawl on hot coal tar
road; Sisters drugged as sex slaves
Student leaders bayoneted at checkpoints
Newspapers houses set ablaze
Palm kernels filled our food shelves

Foreigners looted our treasures
Our flag draped in bloodstains
The face of Africa's pride bowed in shame
As smokes told our stories of carnage
Brothers, lay down the wedding gowns
Discard the scary wigs, sisters, come home

Mothers and fathers,
give these children a hug
A haunted force ruled this space
and broke our spines
But our souls kept moving
The voices of all our sons,
Left to die on the roadside,
Those abandoned in houses
Too sick to move
Those whose fate
the commandos held
at checkpoints
The voices swept
at massacres
those slayed
by pointed fingers

Rest in peace, brothers,
Rest in peace, sisters,
Rest in peace, mothers
Rest in peace, fathers
Sleep tight!
Your baby, Liberia,
will live again…

COMING SOON!!!!
A TEASER

Bonus

Note to a Virgin,

My dear Gbaingah,
When you step outside those walls,
beware the Sun and Stars their
smiles sit on a pit
don't trust the warmth
of their arms they carry
a furnace beneath

When men call you sisters,
keep an eye awake
moments do fade
and your brother could be a villain
tearing your walls to pieces as you
kneel in tears
picking up the shreds left of yourself
wallowing in the bosom of grief

Keep your pearl like a flame in the wind It's
the compass that lights your way When a
man tells you how your lips glow and writes
a check for a feel of your gold trust the
time of the day and keep moving.

When your steel is broken,
you'll sweep the bottom
of the Ocean in search of your suitor.

For the Girl Child…

My power is me
I can roar at a lion
and tear him apart
if I believe the spear
in my voice can slit its neck
and the sword in my eyes
can break his backs
My voice has a radiation
that melts the sun away
I gave away my power
if I lose my voice
I spill it in a fountain
of hopelessness
Staring as it washes
away with the stream
I've met abuse I've met rape
I've met domestic violence
I've met marginalization They
tried to smash my world and
take my power
But I got it back and placed
it in a showcase of hope
I rose from hell with my pride
fastened in my fist
I've remained…

ABOUT THE AUTHOR

Lekpele M. Nyamalon is a Telecommunications and Marketing Professional with over a decade experience in the Telecommunications Industry.

He is an OSIWA Poetry fellow, a 2015 winner of the Young People deserve World Poetry Day competition, an essayist, writer and a Pan Africanist.

Lekpele is the founder of Africa's Life - an afro centric youth based non-profit organisation that inspires youth through motivational speaking and Arts & Culture.

His debut collection of poetry, 'Yearnings of a Traveler' was an Amazon #1 best seller.

www.ingramcontent.com/pod-product-compliance
Lightning Source LLC
Chambersburg PA
CBHW032134040426
42449CB00005B/233